AF148451

Using storytelling to talk about...

Managing feelings & Behaviour

Stories, Poems and Activities to teach and learn in the Early Years

Contents

POEM
STORY
POEM
STORY
SONG
STORY
POEM
STORY

Published by Practical Pre-School Books, A Division of MA Education Ltd, St Jude's Church, Dulwich Road, Herne Hill, London, SE24 0PB.
Tel: 020 7738 5454 www.practicalpreschoolbooks.com

© MA Education Ltd 2022

Design: Mary Holmes fonthillcreative 01722 717036

All images © MA Education Ltd. with the exception of border images; p5 © Afanasia/Adobe Stock; p11-12 © Ayamap/Adobe Stock; p29 © thruer/ Adobe Stock; p35-36 © zera93/Adobe Stock & brgfx/Adobe Stock; p41 © ann131313.a/Adobe Stock; p47-48 © ssstocker/Adobe Stock.

ISBN 978-1-912611-34-8

Introduction

About the series

This book is part of the 'Using storytelling to talk about...' series which gives teaching practitioners the support and resources to develop and use storytelling and poetry/song performance skills in the Early Years Foundation Stage. Each book has specifically-written short interactive stories and poems/songs that are linked to the three different learning and development areas, 'Personal, social and emotional development', 'Understanding the world' and 'Health and self care'. The prime area 'Communication and language' is a running thread throughout all five books.

How to use the series

All the stories and poems/songs deal with issues or experiences that would be familiar to young children. They are short, interactive and simple to perform, with repetitive texts that offer the children the opportunity to respond and join in at their own level of understanding and language development.

The stories and poems/songs can be used in a variety of ways, for example:
- as a 'Let's have a short story (poem/song)' session at a set time each day or on a particular day of the week.
- as a way to help introduce, support or consolidate a topic or theme.
- by choosing a themed story/poem to support or discuss a particular issue, e.g. sharing.
- as an assembly or class performance resource.
- as a book corner recording for play sessions or quiet time.

How to use this book

This book contains eight themed sections that are linked to different early learning goals listed in the focused learning and development area. Each section has a story or a poem icon to show what type of text it is. Use the contents page to select the theme or type of text that you require.

Each section is divided into the following parts:

A. Teacher's notes

- **Theme name:** main learning skill or idea focus behind the story or poem/song and accompanying activities.
- **EYFS learning objectives:** relevant early learning goals from the book's main learning and development area.
- **What you need:** list of resources such as props, images/pictures, puppets and resource sheets.

Before the story or poem/song
- **Getting ready:** tips on what resources to collect, prepare and have ready in advance.
- **Introducing the story or poem/song:** suggestions on how to stimulate the children's curiosity and imagination about the theme, story or poem, e.g. telling and sharing an experience, introducing a character puppet and using props or images.
- **Performance suggestions:** suggestions on how to tell or perform a story or poem/song, e.g. body movements, use of voice and child participation ideas.

After the story or poem/song
These two parts are designed as springboards for further exploration and discussion about the story or poem/song as well as its theme. They could be carried out straight after the story or poem/rhyme or over several days or weeks.
- **Ideas to reinforce the theme:** discussion ideas, activities and question examples to help consolidate the children's understanding and response to the story or poem/song and its main theme.
- **Consolidation activities:** interactive activities to reinforce the story or poem/song and its theme, e.g. using puppets, circle games, music, performance ideas, role play, parachute games and display suggestions.

B. The story or poem/song texts

Body and voice actions suggestions are included for some of the stories and poems/songs. As you get to know the stories and poems/songs, you may want to add in your own ideas and actions.

C. Related activities within the learning environment

A mix of child-led and adult–led cross-curricular activities relating to the story or poem/song and its theme. The activities can be carried out within activity stations, play or in specific learning sessions. Areas include: literacy, mathematics, art and craft, environment, small world play.

D. Resource sheets

Most of the stories and poems/songs have character or picture images. These can be copied onto card, laminated and used as puppets or as story support. Other resource sheets include games, activity cards or templates.

Other resources

Storytelling and performance evaluation record
Use this record to self-evaluate your storytelling skills and performance after each of the stories and poems/songs and for future sessions.

Observation suggestions and chart
Use 'Observation suggestions' and 'Observation chart' as an assessment guide to help you identify and note the developing skills, knowledge and attitudes of individuals or groups of children.

Preparation

One of the most important elements of story telling and poem/song performance is good preparation. Areas to consider before you see the children are:

1. Choosing a place to read or perform

Choose a comfortable and spacious area to tell stories or perform poems and songs. This could be in a book corner or a place where there is a big rug for the children to sit on. Make sure that there is room for the children to move if they will need to use body actions.

2. Look, read and learn the texts

a. Reading the text - If you prefer to read the text to the children, practise reading it out loud several times on your own. Note any need for voice intonation and expression and simple body actions as well as repetitive words or phrases that the children could join in with you.

b. Learning a story or poem/song

- Read the story or poem/song out loud to yourself several times so you get to know the plot, characters, actions, voices and repetitive texts.
- Split the story or verses into easy sections to learn off by heart.
- You don't have to learn it exactly word for word but try and learn the repetitive text and choruses.
- Story memory aid: Have the skeleton of the story with the main repetitive words/phrases by your side or put it into a 'prompt envelope'. If you forget the story, tell the children that a character has sent you a letter or card about what happened next.
- Poem/song memory aid: Have the verses on a sheet of paper near you or add the verses onto the storyboard so you can read them if needed.

c. Props

Use props to introduce a story or poem/song, enhance the telling and message, encourage interactive participation by the children or aid discussion after the telling.

Prepare or collect your props before the session and plan out how they will be used. Have them close at hand and if possible away from the children's reach. If you need to show a number of props then make sure they are laid out in the right order so that you don't need to work out where each one is while you are performing.

When selecting props, think about the story or poem/song and decide which props would work well, e.g. a bucket and spade for a sandcastle story.

d. A special story and rhyme basket/box

Have a story basket (e.g. picnic hamper) or a box with a lid in which to store the props suggested in the story or poem/song. Over time, the children will become eager to find out what is in the basket/box for that session. Keep them guessing or offer little clues, e.g. In the basket is something we can use to build sandcastles. What is it?

e. Story board - a visual aid

Some young children find visual images help reinforce story events or characters. These are especially useful for children who speak English as a second language. One way to do this, is to have a good sized storyboard in which you can attach pictures and characters (see Resource Sheets) before and during the performance or telling. Attach a sticky backing so they can stick easily onto the board.

2. Starting the session

Develop a routine where the children know that it is story time or poem/song time. Make sure children with sight or hearing disabilities are near to you and if possible, have adult support on hand for children with physical or learning difficulties.

Start with a simple rhythm or chant as a clear signal that it's time for stories or poems and songs, e.g. a clapping rhythm, word sounds or 'Time to sit, time to listen. 1-2-3 it's story time!'

Introducing the story or poem/song

It is important to engage the children's imagination and curiosity before you start telling your story or poem/song, e.g. a related prop such as baked bread for exploring senses; introducing a character image or puppet; using an image to encourage discussion or make up a small story about your own life that links to the story or poem/ song theme.

Performance skills

A storyteller can use a range of different methods to tell a story or perform a poem or song to a young audience. These include:

- speaking slowly and clearly to a point behind the group so that all the children can hear you
- looking around the group while you perform so that every child feels involved
- using different voice tone to distinguish between different characters and their moods, as well as highlighting sound effects, actions and events
- using body actions to illustrate movements and expressions
- using a small number of props
- involving the children where possible, e.g. join in with actions, words, sounds
- improvising the text or actions if you can't remember the words or in response to the children's involvement or reactions
- positively acknowledging any interruptions and then weaving back to the story.
- revisiting the story or poem/song several times so that the children recognise it and join in with words and phrases.

The most important thing is to enjoy, share and have fun with the stories, poems and songs!

Theme: Recognising and dealing with feelings

EYFS learning outcomes

To understand how we can:
- talk about how we and others show feelings
- talk about our own and others' behaviour

What you need:

- Our special story and rhyme basket/box' (optional)
- 'My Different Feelings' – poem
- Story board (optional)
- 'Recognising feelings' cards Resource sheet 1 (RS1)
- 'Coping with feelings 'cards – Resource sheet 2 (RS2)
- 'Masks template' – Resource sheet 3 (RS3)

Getting ready:

Prepare a mask from Masks template – RS3 for introducing the poem. Copy and cut out 'Recognising feelings' cards – RS1 and 'Coping with feelings' cards – RS2. You may want to display them on the story board or invite children to hold them up.

Introducing the poem

This poem looks at five examples of moods/feelings that most children would relate to. Show the children the mask and put it across your eyes. Ask the children to work out how you are feeling by looking at the expression of your mouth and body actions. Use some or all of the five feelings in the poem.

Performance suggestions

Before you read out or perform a verse, place the relevant feeling from 'Recognising feelings' cards – RS1 on the story board or invite a child to hold it up. Use intonation and body language to illustrate each mood feeling at the start of a verse. Read out/perform the last two lines in a positive, upbeat tone. Display the matching positive images from 'Coping with feelings' cards – RS2. Read/perform a couple of times and encourage the children to mime along with the actions and facial expressions.

Ideas to reinforce theme

- Use the 'Recognising feelings' cards – RS1 and 'Coping with feelings' cards – RS2 to discuss the different scenarios. For younger children, put the matching cards together. Point to a 'Recognising feelings' card and ask what the child is feeling and why. Point to the matching card and discuss how the child deals with his/her feeling. Mix up the matching cards for older children and encourage them to work out what goes with what.

- After the poem, ask: *Which one of these feelings have you felt today?* Be aware of and sensitive to the children's experiences as you ask the questions. Volunteer your own experiences of feelings. Work positively, with the children to think of simple ways to help cope with the four feelings. Talk about positive feelings too, e.g. happy, excited, calm etc.

Consolidation activities

Puppet
Use a puppet to act out a familiar scenario or share an experience about how it felt about an occasion, e.g. nervous about swimming. Encourage children to give advice and help to the puppet on ways it could deal with the feeling, e.g. take a breath, ask for help etc. Highlight how children can always ask for help in dealing with feelings they don't like.

Circle game
Use a mask from Masks template – RS3. Pass the mask round the circle to a simple rhythmic beat. Once the beat stops, the child with the mask puts it over their eyes and make an expression using their body and lower part of their face to illustrate a mood. The others have to guess what it is. End the game with everyone counting to 3 and making a happy face.

Display idea
Take photographs of the children each making a face for a different feelings. Enlarge the faces and place their decorated masks (see Art and Craft) and display with mood /feeling words under each one.

My Different Feelings

When Sue is feeling angry,
She wants to scream and shout,
But when she counts from one to ten,
Her anger all comes out.

When Hoe is feeling grumpy,
He wants to stamp and cry,
But when he tries to smile and grin,
His grumpy mood goes by.

When Jade is feeling sad,
She wants to stop her tears,
So when she gets a lovely hug,
Her sadness disappears.

When Naz is feeling nervous,
He wants to hide away,
But when he takes a big deep breath,
His worries float away.

When Mel is feeling happy,
She wants to laugh and play,
So when she goes and sees her friends,
She smiles and smiles all day.

Related activities within the learning environment

Literacy

Discuss words that describe moods. Write them down as the children say them. You will be amazed how many words they can find for just one mood.

Work with a group to create one or two more extra verses for the feelings poem using the same structure as the 'My Different Feelings'. Write it down as you go along.

Mathematics

Practise counting up to 20. If the group is confident in their counting, try counting backwards from 20 to 0.

Art & Craft

Give each child a card mask from 'Masks template' – RS3 to decorate in bright colours or materials. Attach sticks to them and let the children use them in class activities or their own play activities.

Leave out materials or show children how to create a calm-inducing item e.g. a soft toy, a soft chiming mobile or gentle sounding cardboard tube rainstick.

Music

Leave out a range of musical instruments and encourage the children to investigate making different sounds to depict different types of feelings/moods. They could perform their ideas to the class or to a group of friends.

Provide music for the children to listen to that could represent different moods. What music makes them feel happy or sad? Why?

ICT

Show a children's film/cartoon version of Sergei Prokofiev's 'Peter and the Wolf'. Discuss Peter's changes in feelings in the story.

Games

Copy and laminate one or two sets of 'Recognising feelings' cards – RS1 and 'Coping with feelings' cards – RS2. Let pairs of children use them to play matching games/pairs or create their own stories from the different scenarios.

'Recognising feelings' cards

Copy and cut out cards.

Use for discussion and game activities.

Resource sheet 2

'Coping with feelings' cards

Copy and cut out cards.

Use for discussion and
game activities.

Masks template

Copy and cut out.

Attach sticks to hold
mask to face.

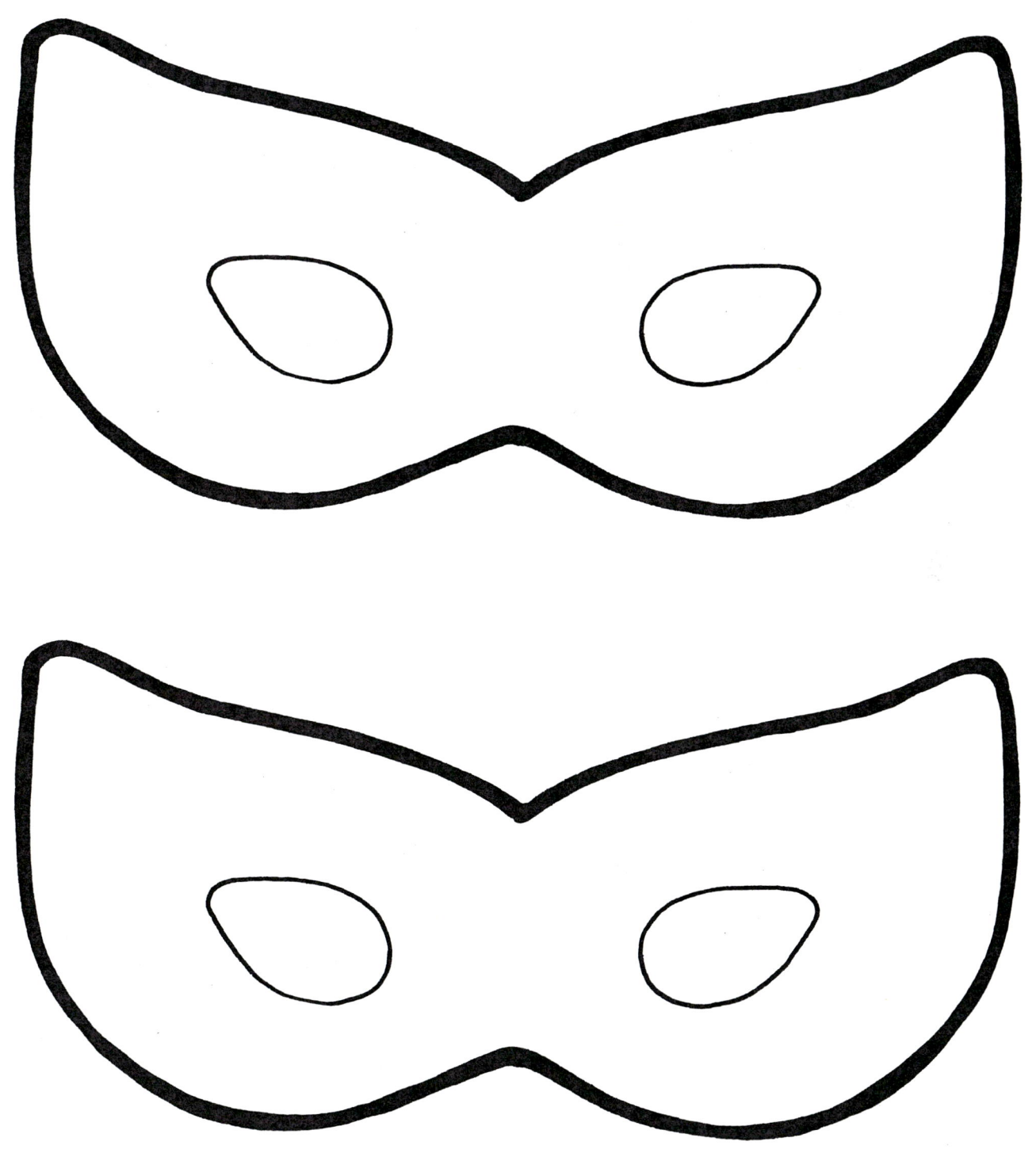

Theme: Losing something

What you need:

- Our special story and rhyme basket/box' (optional)
- I've Lost My Blanket –story
- Story board (optional)
- A blanket
- Story characters 1 – Resource sheet 1 (RS1)
- Story characters 2– Resource sheet 2 (RS2)

Getting ready:

Have a small blanket or cloth available (or put it in 'Our special short story and rhyme box'). If you want to show the story characters, copy out the images from 'Story characters 1' – RS1 and 'Story characters 2' – RS2 You may want to display them on the story board or invite children to hold them up as stick puppets.

Introducing the story

Show the children an object that you like very much. Create a little monologue about how you thought you had lost it and looked everywhere. You felt sad but then you found it again. Show the children the blanket or cloth and highlight how it reminds you of a story of Little Prince who once lost his favourite blanket. Read or perform the story.

Performance suggestions

If you want to display the characters, place them on the story board in story order. Point to each character in turn as you read the story. If you are performing the story, you may want to use puppets. Use different voices for the characters. Encourage the children to join in with Little Prince's repetitive crying chorus each time it comes up in the story.

Ideas to reinforce theme

- Discuss the story with the children using the story images if possible. Ask: *Why did Little Prince love his blanket so much? How did he feel when he lost his blanket? (let's repeat the chorus). Why did another blanket make him happy again?* Look at the other ways people tried to make Little Prince happy. Ask: *Which one would make you happy again?*

- Encourage the children to share their experiences of having a special toy or comforter when they were younger and why they liked it. Invite any children to share their experience of losing something special. Highlight to the children that although it can be very sad to lose something, there will be other things that can be special later on.

Consolidation activities

Puppets
Make story puppets by attaching sticks onto the 'Story characters 1 and 2' (RS1 and RS2). Encourage the children to use the puppets as you slowly retell the story to the class. As a group/class, think of new suggestions by the characters of ways to make Little Prince happy again.

Role play
Put the children into twos or threes. Pretend you have lost a sock and not sure where it is. Let the groups of children think of a place where it could be, e.g. under the bed, in the wash basket etc. They could share their location suggestion and everyone mimes looking for it or they could mime the action and the rest of the children guess where they are looking.

Circle game
Ask the children how they could make Little Prince happy again. Model an example, e.g. '*I would … (tell him a story/ give him a sock puppet)*. The children can answer individually, or discuss it with the child next to them before you start going round the circle. After each one, model saying 'Thank you. You are very kind.'

I've Lost My Blanket!

Once there was a little prince who lived in a big castle with his mother and father, the king and queen.

Little Prince had many toys but the one thing that he loved most of all was his old baby blanket. It didn't look very special but it went everywhere with Little Prince. When he was tired or not sure of things, he would cuddle his blanket and feel safe and warm.

One morning Little Prince woke up and found that his blanket had gone! He sat on his bed and started to cry.

"Oh, no! Our Little Prince is crying," said the queen. "Something terrible must have happened."

The king and queen quickly ran across the castle to Little Prince's bedroom.

"What's the matter, Little Prince?" asked the king.

Little Prince took a deep breath and cried,

"I've lost my blanket. I've lost my blanket. Please find my blanket, now!"

The king and queen ordered everyone in the castle to look for the blanket. They looked high and they looked low but the blanket was nowhere to be seen.

The king and queen didn't like Little Prince to be sad. How could they make him happy again?

The castle's cook had an idea.

"When I was a little boy, " he said, "my cuddly teddy bear made me feel happy."

The king quickly ran to the toy shop and bought the cuddliest teddy bear he could find.

Surely this would help Little Prince forget about his blanket and feel happy again!

But as soon as he saw the teddy, Little Prince took a deep breath and cried,

"I've lost my blanket. I've lost my blanket. Please find my blanket, now!"

The castle gardener came to the king and queen.

"When I was a little girl," she said, "my mother used to sing to make me happy."

"That's a good idea, exclaimed the queen and so she started to sing Little Prince's favourite song. Let's help her and join in too."

I've Lost My Blanket!

Here we go round the Mulberry Bush,

The Mulberry Bush,

The Mulberry Bush.

Here we go round the Mulberry Bush,

On a cold and frosty morning.

But guess what! That didn't work either. Little Prince just cried and cried,

"I've lost my blanket. I've lost my blanket. Please find my blanket, now!"

Soon the castle was full of people trying to think of different ways to make Little Prince feel happy again, now that he had lost his special blanket. They gave him dummies, soft ribbons, a fun pet, a delicious apple pie and even a new wool blanket from the local shepherd boy and his sheep - but nothing worked.

All Little Prince wanted was his old blanket back.

Soon it was time for bed, The queen gave little Prince a big hug and wiped away his tears.

"Don't worry, Little Prince," she said. "Perhaps we will find it in the morning."

Little Prince liked being held in his mother's arms. It made him feel safe and warm, just like his old blanket. Soon he felt sleepy.

As he lay down he noticed a lump under his pillow. He put his hand under the pillow and found – can you guess? His old blanket!

He jumped out of bed and shouted happily,

"I've found my blanket! I've found my blanket! I have my blanket now."

The king and queen were overjoyed, the cook was overjoyed, the gardener was overjoyed, the villagers were overjoyed, even the sheep were overjoyed – baaaa!

And Little Prince?

Well - he snuggled down into his old soft, cosy, baby blanket and went fast asleep.

Related activities within the learning environment

Literacy

Ask the children to draw a new comforter for Little Prince. Write the name of the object under the drawing or encourage the children to write it themselves.

Leave out card and writing materials for the children to create thank you cards from Little Prince. Encourage the children to trace over the words and write their own names.

Mathematics

Encourage sorting and shape recognition skills by giving the children a pile of different shaped and sized cloth to organise into similar shapes or sizes. The cloth could also be sorted into colour or textures.

Art & Craft

Make decorated boxes that can be used to store special toys or objects so they don't get lost. Let the children cover them with different materials and/or paint.

Let the children use fabric pens to decorate a square shaped cloth with the image of their favourite object or comforter. Display the cloths for the children to see.

Games

In small groups or pairs, the children look closely at an object (real or photo). Discuss its size, colour, what's on it, what it's used for etc. Now hide the photo and ask children describe the object to you.

Create pairs of cards showing a person and their matching item, e.g. post deliverer – letter, builder – hammer, gardener – plant pot, dancer – shoe, baby – pram. Ask the children to match the missing items to the right person.

Role play corner

Set up a lost property office. Put out boxes of 'lost' items like clothes, umbrellas and toys. Encourage the children to think of different ways of sorting the items so they can be found easily,

Resource sheet 1

Use the story characters as pictures or puppets
or laminate to use in the story corner.

Little Prince

Little Prince

Queen

King

Story characters 2

Use the story characters as pictures or puppets
or laminate to use in the story corner.

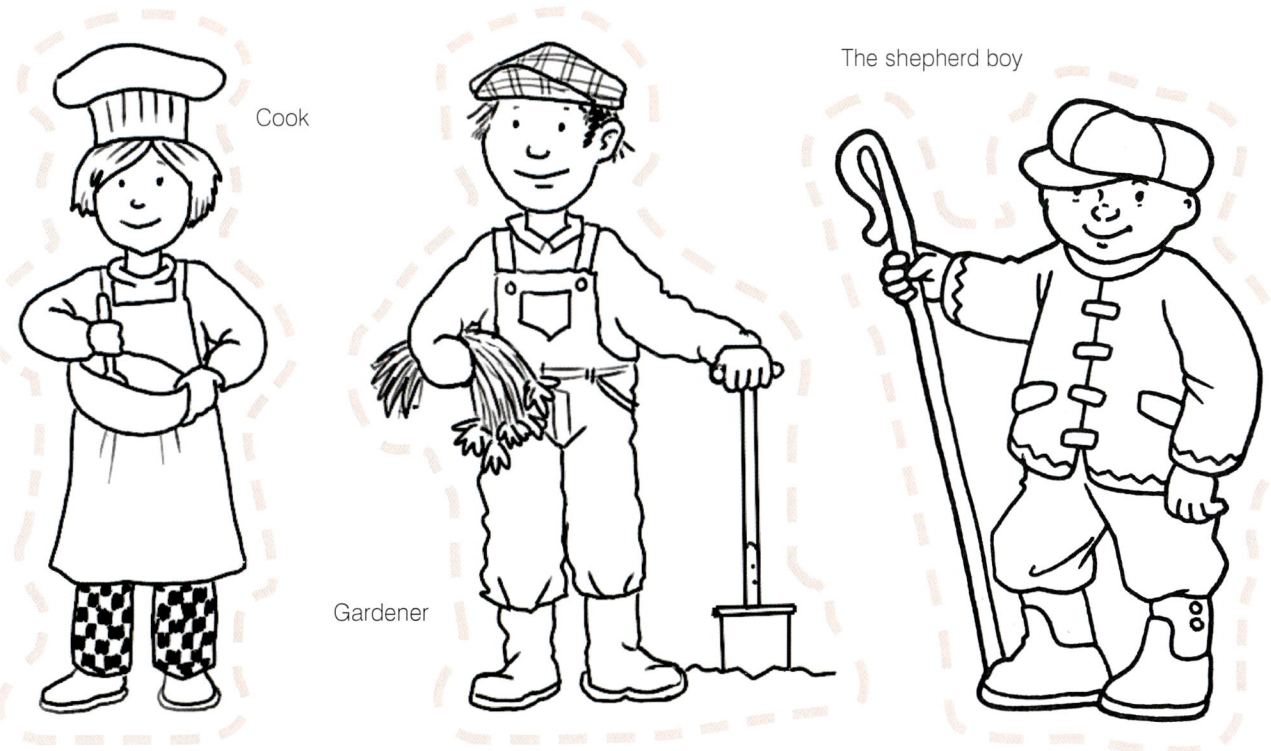

Cook

Gardener

The shepherd boy

The villagers

Theme: Feeling scared

EYFS learning outcomes

To understand how we can:
- talk about how we and others show feelings
- adjust our behaviour to different situations

What you need:

- Our special story and rhyme basket/box' (optional
- There's a Monster Under The Bed – rhyme
- Story board (optional)
- 'Poem picture cards – Resource sheet 1 (RS1)
- 'Overcoming fear' cards – Resource sheet 2 (RS2)
- 'Happy/scared faces' – Resource sheet 3 (RS3)

Getting ready:

Prepare a 'Happy/scared faces' – RS3 and have them available (or put it in 'Our special short story and rhyme box'). Copy the 'Poem picture cards' – RS1 if you want to show the images while you read or perform the poem. Display them on the story board or where the children can clearly see them.

Introducing the poem

Show the children the two masks. Say: *This is how I feel and look when I feel a little scared about something* (hold up scared mask) *but this is how I feel when I'm not scared anymore* (happy mask). Explain that you are going to tell the children a poem about being scared of certain things and ways not to be scared about them anymore.

Performance suggestions

If you display the poem picture cards, point to each picture in turn while you read or perform each verse. You could also use the masks to highlight the negative and positive reactions in the poem. Encourage the children to join in with the repetitive words '*Oh no!*' and '*Oh yes!*'. Put emphasis on the word '*So...*' to highlight the change of confidence in dealing with a frightening experience. Use scared and then a happy sounding voice and hand/arm movements for the different actions.

Ideas to reinforce theme

- Display the six scary scenarios from 'Poem picture cards' – RS1 in verse order. Read or perform the first three scary lines of a verse. Ask: *What did the child decide to do to stop themselves being less scared?* Place the happy image by the scary image, Encourage the children to think of different ways they could be less scared in the same situation, e.g. turning monsters into comical characters.

- Display the 'Overcoming fear cards' – RS2. Look at each of the four images that show a child being scared about a situation. Discuss the situation and encourage the children to think of ways the child can help deal with it. Display the matching card and discuss why they are good actions. Point to the girl who asks an adult for help. Ask: *Who could you ask for help if you were scared of something?* (teacher, helper, friend, family, carer).

Consolidation activities

Puppets
Use a puppet to come across as scared. Ask the puppet what it is scared of and encourage the children to volunteer ideas to help it feel better and deal with its fears. Use several examples that the children could relate to in their own lives, e.g. dark, noise, busy road etc. Show the puppet getting less scared and more happier during the talk. Thank the children for their help.

Role play
Let the children use their faces and bodies to mime the different scenarios in each verse of the poem as you recite it out loud. They could also join in with the repetitive '*oh, no*' '*oh, yes*' and '*so*'. If needed, model how to use your body and face to show a braver happier person at the end of each verse. Add more scenarios with the children.

Display idea
On one side of the display board, have pictures and images of things that the children have said they are frightened of. On the other side of the board have pictures of positive ways of dealing with the frightening issues. Link the images with pieces of string so the children can connect the two.

There's a Monster under My Bed

There's a monster under my bed. Oh no!
There's a monster under my bed.

So… I will tell it to go away. Oh yes!
On a monster holiday.

The fireworks are getting too loud. Oh no!
The fireworks are getting too loud.

So… I will wipe away my tears. Oh yes!
And cover up my ears.

My mummy and daddy have gone. Oh no!
My mummy and daddy have gone.

So… I will hold my teacher's hand. Oh yes!
And build castles in the sand.

There's a spider in the bath. Oh no!
There's a spider in the bath.

So… I will ask my Granny Dee, Oh yes!
To go and set it free.

There's a big dog barking at me. Oh no!
There's a big dog barking at me.

So… I will hold my head up high, Oh yes!
And walk on slowly by.

My mummy has turned off the light. Oh no!
My mummy has turned off the light.

So… I will find my cuddly sheep, Oh yes!
And sing myself to sleep.

Related activities within the learning environment

Literacy

Collect and display a selection of picture books about overcoming fear for the children to look at and share.

Record the poem for the children to listen to and join in. Have a laminated set of the 'Poem picture cards' – RS1 for the children to look at and sort while listening to the poem.

Mathematics

Use nursery rhymes such as '*What's the time. Mr Wolf?*' to explore the use of mathematical language e.g. 'o'clock', numbers of steps. Use '*Little Miss Muffet*' to count the number of spider legs on the spider.

Art & Craft

Let the children create funny pictures of monsters by painting an unusual shape down one half of the paper, folding it over to make a mirror image shape. Draw in eyes, arms, legs or use materials to give an individual look. Let the children choose names for their monster.

Make a simple dream catchers and hang them around the classroom. Explain that some North American Native Indian tribes used them to catch bad dreams.

ICT

Show short films for the children to watch about creatures that they might be scared up so they can learn more about them, e.g. spiders, snakes, dogs.

Games

Give group of children, 'Happy/scared faces' – RS3. Shuffle the 'Poem picture cards' – RS1 and 'Overcoming fear cards' – RS2 and place them face down in middle of table/floor. Each child takes turns to show top card to group. They all use their happy or scared face to show what is shown.

Small world

Put out small world figures and sets to encourage children to act out imaginary scenarios of their characters overcoming a scary situation or helping others who are scared.

Poem picture cards

Copy and cut the cards to use for discussion, activities and the story corner.

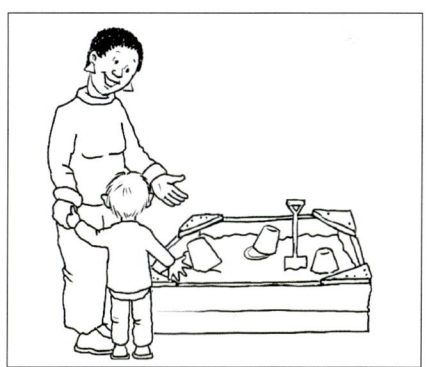

Resource sheet 2

'Overcoming fear' cards

Match the pictures.

'Happy/scared faces

Copy and cut out for activities, Attach a stick to the faces to make masks.

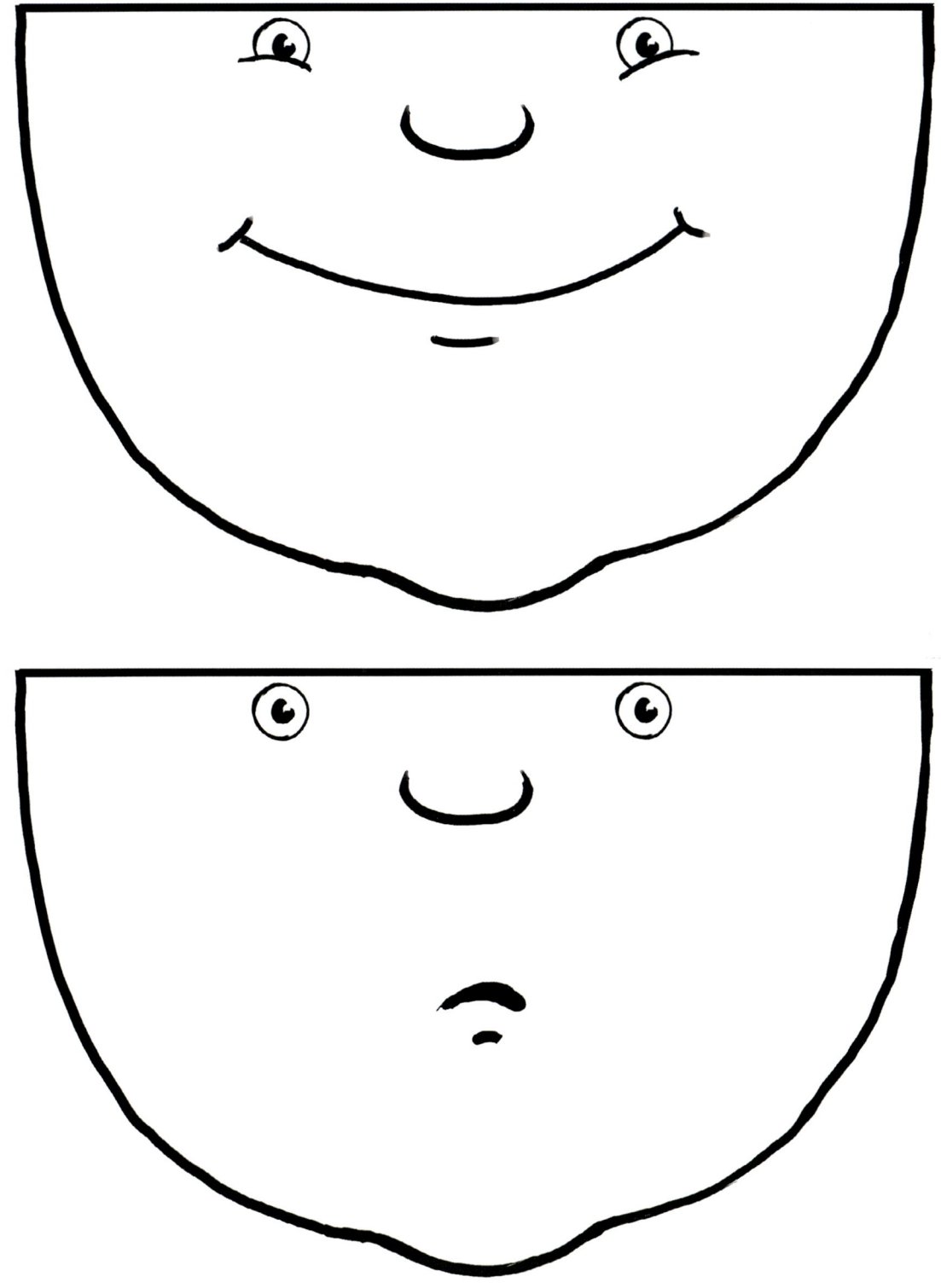

Theme: Being a good friend

What you need:

- Our special story and rhyme basket/box' (optional)
- Hyena's Loud Laugh – story
- Story board (optional)
- 'Hyena story characters' – Resource sheet 1 (RS1)
- 'Friendship figure template' – Resource sheet 2 (RS2)

Getting ready:

Have an image of Hyena from 'Hyena story characters' – RS1 available (or put it in the 'Our special story and poem basket/box). Have a simple joke available.

Introducing the story

Introduce the children to Hyena –as a picture on the story board or as a stick puppet. Explain that when she finds something funny, she laughs and laughs. Do an example of the laugh. Highlight that she also likes her friends. Ask the children why Hyena might like her friends. Explain that you are going to tell a story about the one time, when her friends made her sad.

Performance suggestions

When you make a hyena laugh, be aware of any children in the group who may be sensitive to loud sounds. Use different voices for each of the animal characters.

Ideas to reinforce theme

- Discuss the story with the children. Ask: *How did Elephant and Monkey upset Hyena? Why were they not very good friends to Hyena? Why do you think Hyena didn't want to laugh again? How did they help Hyena laugh again?* Invite the children to tell a joke that would make Hyena and her friends laugh.

- Ask the children what they like about their friends. Discuss what a good friend is – caring, helpful, kind, fun, sharing things etc. Share examples of when friends are upset or cross with each other. Highlight how being friends means that you forgive each other and play together again, e.g. by saying sorry, hugging, starting a new game or sharing something special.

Consolidation activities

Puppets
Make stick puppets of the three characters from 'Hyena story characters' – RS1 to retell the story. Let the children take turns operating the puppets and telling the jokes. Encourage the children to add the hyena laugh. Extend the story, using the puppets, by thinking of other stories about how one of the animals annoys the others and they fall out, then make up again.

Role play
Put the children into pairs (friend pairs if appropriate). Ask one to make movements and the other to copy as if looking in the mirror. Start with facial expressions and extend it to body movements and then miming an action of an activity they like doing as friends. Swap round.

Circle game
Put the children into a circle and play 'Pass a friendship handshake'. Start by shaking hands with a child who gets up and shakes another person in the circle and so on. Extend the activity by passing on a smile or a hello.

Display idea
Display the children's friendship figures made in an arts and craft session by linking each one to make a friendship chain.

Hyena's Loud Laugh

Once upon a time there lived a hyena who loved to laugh. Everything seemed funny to her.

She laughed at the way the little ants ran backwards and forwards all day long. She laughed at the way the sun came up in the morning and went down at night. She laughed at the way Elephant used his long trunk to splash mud on his back, and she laughed at the way Monkey used his long arms to swing from tree to tree.

Now you might think that Hyena was a fun animal to have around – always happy, always jolly – but her friends didn't think so. The main problem was the sound of her laugh…

AAAA-HEEEEEEEEE! AAAA-HEEEEEEEEEE!

…it was so **loud**!

Her friends liked Hyena very much, but her loud laughing would often gave them headaches or made it difficult to have a nice long snooze in the warm sun.

One morning, Monkey and Elephant woke up to silence. For some reason Hyena was not laughing – everything was so peaceful and quiet. They were just sitting down to a breakfast when Hyena walked miserably by.

"Good morning, Hyena," called out Elephant. "You're very quiet this morning. Anything wrong?"

"I think I've lost my laugh," sighed Hyena sadly. "I woke up, looked at my funny face in the water, opened my mouth to laugh and all I heard was this… **hic, hic, hic.**

I miss my laugh. It makes me feel happy. Will you help me find it?"

Elephant and Monkey looked at each other and in one big voice said, **"No!"**

"We'd rather spend our time enjoying the peace and quiet," said Monkey.
"and it's so much better now we don't have to listen to that loud laugh of yours," yawned Elephant.

Hyena felt sad and upset. She thought her friends liked her laugh. With her head down, she walked slowly back to her cave.

For several days, Elephant and Monkey enjoyed life without the sound of Hyena's loud laugh – they had picnics, slept and caught flies. But after a while they started feeling restless – it was beginning to feel too quiet.

Hyena's Loud Laugh

"I wonder when Hyena will pop by to say hello, " said Monkey, one day. "It feels odd not having her around or hearing that loud laugh. I actually miss hearing it."

Elephant lifted her long trunk to scratch the top of her head. "We weren't very nice to Hyena," she said glumly. "I've been thinking of a way to help her find her laugh and I've got just the thing."

Later that day, they walked over to Hyena's cave and knocked nervously.
Hyena came out looking cross and fed-up. "What do you want?" she snapped. "I thought you didn't like me or my loud laugh."
"We're sorry," said Elephant. "We didn't mean it. We miss your laugh and we miss you. So we've come to help you get your laugh back."
"By telling you our best and funniest jokes," giggled Monkey.

Hyena sat back and sighed. She wasn't in the mood for silly jokes. Elephant was first.

> What's grey, has four legs and jumps up and down?
>
> An elephant on a trampoline.

Monkey howled with laughter,
hoooo haaaa hoooo haaaa

...but Hyena didn't laugh - she just looked sadly at the ground.

Next came Monkey's joke.

> What does a monkey call his Grandmother?
>
> A ban-nana!

Elephant's whole body shook with laughter…
ehhhhhhhhhhhhhh!

…but Hyena was still silent.

The two friends were just wondering what joke to tell next, when they heard a strange sound that seemed to be getting louder and louder and louder!

Aaaa-heeeeeeeeee Aaaa-heeeeeeeeee AAAA-HEEEEEEEEE

Hyena had got her lovely loud laugh back. Her friends were overjoyed and told each other jokes until the sun went down.

And Monkey and Elephant learnt never to be mean to a good friend again.

Related activities within the learning environment

Literacy

The children can make friendship cards by either writing or making marks inside ready-made cards or using card and materials.

Let the children make a friendship booklet – give them a booklet where they can draw and if able, write a simple sentence on favourite activities with friends.

Mathematics

Encourage pairs of children to work well together to sort out mathematical problems such as completing a pattern, counting money or sorting shapes.

Art & Craft

Let the children create friendship bracelets or friendship badges that they can give to a friend. Bracelets could be made by threading colourful beads onto pipe cleaners. Badges could be decorated onto round card which is then laminated.

Give the children a copy of 'Friendship figure template' – RS3 and let them decorate it for a friend. Discuss what colours or materials that friend may like. Display them in a chain around the room.

ICT

Collect jokes from the children and write them out on the computer. Invite each child to select their own font size and style as well as adding clipart imagery. Print out the jokes and put them in a book. Record the children saying the jokes so they can hear and enjoy them.

Exploring

Arrange activities that encourage pairs of children to play and investigate together, such as measuring water for filling up different containers, making a construction model or caring for a class pet or plants.

Display a map of UK or of the world. Work with the children to add images of family and friends with string/thread linking images and names to the location.

Resource sheet 1

Stick a copy of this sheet to card.

Cut out each character and attach a stick to the back so it can be used as a puppet.

Friendship figure template

Theme: Waiting your turn

EYFS learning outcomes

To understand how we can:
- work as part of a group or class
- understand and follow the rules.
- adjust our behaviour to different situations

What you need:

- Our special story and rhyme basket/box' (optional)
- Five Hungry Pirates – song
- Story board (optional)
- 'Waiting at the bus stop' – Resource sheet 1 (RS1)
- 'Five Hungry Pirates' sequencing cards – RS2
- 'Queuing up' – Resource sheet 3 (RS3)

Getting ready:

Have a copy of 'Waiting at the bus stop' – RS1 available (or put it in the 'Our special story and poem basket/box). Copy and cut out the 'Five Hungry Pirates' sequencing cards – RS2. Practise the song and hand actions before you sing it with the children.

Introducing the poem

Show the children the picture 'Waiting at the bus stop' – RS1. Invite any children to read out the sign 'bus stop'. Ask: *What are the people doing?* Point out how they are all queuing and waiting their turn. Talk to the children about situations where they have to line up, such as asking the teacher for help, break time and waiting for drinks. Point out that pushing in or shoving another person in the line is not acceptable. Tell them that the song you are going to sing is about pushing in.

Performance suggestions

Sing this song to the tune of 'Ten Green Bottles'. Use your hands to show five fingers down to 1 finger as you sing each verse. After each verse ask the children how many pirates are left and encourage them to sing along with you. Repeat the song, now the children know what to say and do.

Ideas to reinforce theme

- Display the images from 'Queuing up' – RS1. Look at three pictures which show positive ways of queuing up or being in line, e.g. bus stop, at the supermarket, walking along a road. Talk about why the characters are queuing or walking in line.

- Using 'Queuing up' – RS1, focus on the images of children pushing and shoving into a line/queue. Ask: *How do you think the other children are feeling?* (Suggest they could feel angry, upset or hurt.) *Why do you think we have to stand in lines sometimes?* (Suggest that it makes sure everyone waits their turn fairly, creates less rush and avoids people getting hurt.)

- Encourage children to share experiences of someone pushing or shoving into a queue or line. Ask: *How did you feel? What could you do if someone pushes into a line or pushes you out?* Highlight that children should either explain calmly that everyone is waiting their turn, or arrange for an adult help. Emphasise that children should not push back or start fighting or shouting.

Consolidation activities

Role play
Encourage the children to re-enact 'The Wheels on the Bus' song. Set up bus stops and place them around the room in a circuit. Split the children into groups queuing up at the different bus stop. Invite a child or an adult helper to pretend to drive the bus. Let the bus drive to each stop after a verse and encourage the children at the stop to get on the bus in turn and then follow it around to the next stop.

Display idea
Get the children to draw pictures of themselves. Display the pictures in different queuing scenarios such as waiting at an ice-cream van or bus stop, or lining up for break.

Five Hungry Pirates

(Sing to the tune of 'Ten Green Bottles')

Five hungry pirates, waiting for their tea,
Five hungry pirates, waiting for their tea,
When along came a monkey and pushed one in the sea.
Now there's four hungry pirates, waiting for their tea.

Four hungry pirates, waiting for their tea,
Four hungry pirates, waiting for their tea,
When along came a mermaid and pushed one in the sea.
Now there's three hungry pirates, waiting for their tea.

Three hungry pirates, waiting for their tea,
Three hungry pirates, waiting for their tea,
When along came a walrus and pushed one in the sea.
Now there's two hungry pirates waiting for their tea.

Two hungry pirates, waiting for their tea,
Two hungry pirates, waiting for their tea,
When along came a penguin and pushed one in the sea.
Now there's one hungry pirate waiting for his tea.

One hungry pirate, waiting for his tea,
One hungry pirate, waiting for his tea,
When along came a dolphin, and pushed him in the sea.
Now there's no hungry pirates, waiting for their tea.

No hungry pirates, waiting for their tea,
No hungry pirates, waiting for their tea,
Except the pirate captain, as angry as can be,
For there's no fish and chips for the captain's tea.

Related activities within the learning environment

Literacy

Encourage younger children to explore putting the alphabet letters in the correct order from left to right. Older children can focus on writing words or simple sentences from left to right.

Sing the 'Five Hungry Pirates' with the whole class or small groups. Encourage them to sort out the 'Five Hungry Pirates' sequencing cards – RS2 into the correct sequence order and then re-sing the song again.

Mathematics

Look at number lines. For younger children, have lines up to 10 and encourage them to use the lines to count forwards and backward. Older children can create number lines up to 100.

Art & Craft

Give the children triangular and circular pieces of paper the size of traffic signs. Ask them to draw a picture or symbol to show there should be no pushing in a line.

Music

Sing songs and rhymes using numbers, such as, '*Ten green bottles, Ten in the bed, 1,2,3,4, 5 – once I caught a fish alive.*'

Games

Play straight line team games, e.g. passing a ball over and under, or passing a balloon between, the legs.

Play racing games where the children have to wait for their turn to run.

Visitors & trips

Take the children for a walk. Put them into pairs in a line. Discuss why it is important to stay in a line and not to push or shove along the road.

Role play corner

Set up a supermarket checkout where the children can take turns to pay for food.

Resource sheet 2

Copy and cut out cards for
story sequencing activities.

Using storytelling to talk about…**Managing feelings & Behaviour**

Queuing up

Copy and cut out pictures for discussion activities.

Theme: Learning to Listen

EYFS learning outcomes

To understand how we can:
- talk about our own and others' behaviour and its consequences
- know that some behaviour is unacceptable
- understand and follow the rules

What you need:

- Our special story and rhyme basket/box' (optional)
- 'Listen, Becky Bear' – story
- Story board or a story map of Becky' Bear's journey (optional)
- 'Listen, Becky Bear' characters – Resource sheet 1 (RS1)
- 'What happens next?' – Resource sheet 2 (RS2)

Getting ready:

Copy the images from 'Listen, Becky Bear' characters – RS1'. Display the characters onto the story board or make them into stick puppets. To make it more interesting, create a story map adding the different objects to the route. Move Becky Bear and Daddy Bear along the map as you read the story.

Ideas to reinforce theme

- Discuss the events of the story, using the story images/story map as support. Ask them what Becky's dad told her not to do for each part of the story and what happened when she ignored him. Ask: *Who can retell it back to the class?*

- Discuss different reasons why it is good to listen or take notice of what people are saying to you. Give examples such as, learning how to do something, asking for help, s haring ideas and news with friends and listening to stories.)

Consolidation activities

Puppets
Encourage the children to think of other types of food Becky Bear could collect. Invite them to call out the instructions while you operate the puppet. You could follow the instructions or deliberately ignore them and get into trouble.

Role play
Call out instructions for a fairly simple activity such as washing hands or getting dressed to go outside in bad weather. Encourage the children to listen carefully before acting them out. First, give one instruction at a time, then try calling out all the instructions in one go.

Display idea
Draw a large ear and put it on display. Around the ear, let the children draw different examples of situations where it's good to listen. Add pictures and posters to the display.

Introducing the story

Give simple instructions for the children to follow, e.g. hands on our heads, hands on our knees. Explain to the children that it is very important to listen to instructions. Introduce them to the image or puppet of Becky Bear. Explain how she didn't listen and ended up in trouble.

Performance suggestions

You could read or perform the story without images or story map first and then retell the story using the story map or tell the story with the story map or figure straight away. When you are reading the story, highlight the initial letter sounds of the interrupted words in Dad's instructions. The children could join in with Becky's repeated words to help emphasise that she is not listening.

Listen, Becky Bear

STORY

It was lunch time and Becky Bear was very hungry. Becky's dad went to the cupboard for some food.

"Oh no!" he cried, "We've run out. We'll have to go into the woods and find some more. Would you help me, Becky?"

"Don't worry, Dad," said Becky proudly. "Finding food is easy!"

They picked up a basket and set off into the woods.

Soon they came to a blackberry bush full of juicy blackberries.

"Now, Becky," explained her dad, "when you pick blackberries, you must watch out for the th——"

"I know!" interrupted Becky. "You don't have to tell me. It's easy!"

She stuck both paws into the thorny bush and tried to pick the largest blackberries.

"Ow!" she cried. "The thorns have pricked my paws. They feel really sore!"

"Never mind," sighed her dad. "Let's try to find some honey for our lunch."

Soon they found a bees' nest in a tree.

"Now, Becky," explained her dad, "when you collect honey you must watch out for the b——"

"I know," interrupted Becky. "You don't have to tell me. It's easy!"

She climbed up to the nest and shook it hard. All the bees came out, buzzing angrily.

"Ow!" cried Becky. "The bees have stung my nose. It feels really sore."

Listen, Becky Bear

"Never mind, Becky," sighed her dad. "Let's try to catch some fish for our lunch."

Soon they came to a stream full of wiggling fish. They waded into the middle of the stream and watched the fish swim between their legs.

"Now Becky," explained her dad, "to catch a fish you must stand very st——"

"I know," interrupted Becky. "You don't have to tell me. It's easy!"

She tried to jump on the fish but they were too fast and she fell in the water with a big SPLASH!

"Oh dear!" cried Becky, "I feel very wet and cold."

"Never mind," sighed her dad. "Let's get out of the water and have a rest."

Becky felt very sorry for herself. She was wet, sore and very, very hungry! She looked at her dad and held his paw.

"I'm sorry, Dad," she said unhappily. "I should have listened to you. Will you show me how to get food again?"

So Becky's dad showed her how to catch fish by standing still in the water, showed her how to collect honey without upsetting the bees and showed her how to pick the juiciest blackberries without getting thorns in her paws.

"Wow," said Becky, looking at their full basket. "We've enough food here for a feast!"

"Well done, Becky," smiled her dad. "You've collected us our lunch and you've learned to listen."

Related activities within the learning environment

Literacy

Put the children in pairs or in a small group. Give each child a copy of 'What happens next? – RS2. Look at each scenario and ask the children what they think might happen next. Let them draw or write their ideas at the end of each scenario.

Let the children create their own story map for 'Listen, Becky Bear'. Label the different places and encourage the children to use them in the book corner or as a class.

Mathematics

Give children numeracy instructions, for example: 'Pick up 3 red buttons and 2 blue buttons. How many buttons do you have?'

Give the children beads and thread. Give them instructions for making a particular pattern.

Art & Craft

Give each child a piece of paper. Explain and demonstrate, in stages, how to make a simple paper dart. Stop after each stage and make sure each child is listening. Throw the darts to see if they work.

Exploring

Set up tin can or yogurt pot telephones for the children to use.

Leave out a tape of sound effects. Encourage the children to guess what each effect is.

Music

Start all the children clapping in a steady rhythm. Change the rhythm without warning. The children must copy you once they hear the new rhythm. Keep changing the rhythms to encourage the children to listen.

Sing simple rounds with the children, e.g. *Frère Jacques; London's Burning; A Ram Sam Sam; Head shoulders, knees and toes.*

Games

Play games which involve listening to instructions or messages, e.g. *Chinese whispers, Simon says, Musical statues.*

Environment

Ask the children to look for three, four or five items such as leaves or twigs. Praise them when they bring you the right number.

Resource sheet 1

Copy and cut out pictures for story telling and sequencing activities.

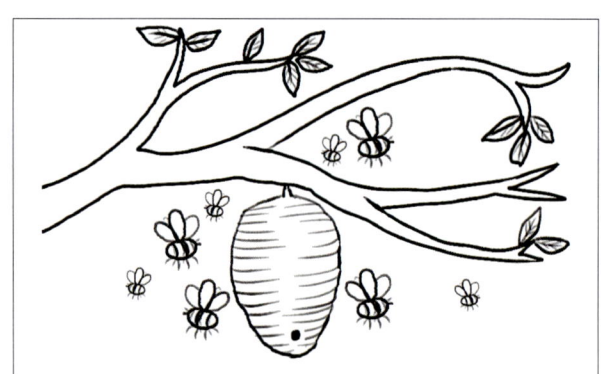

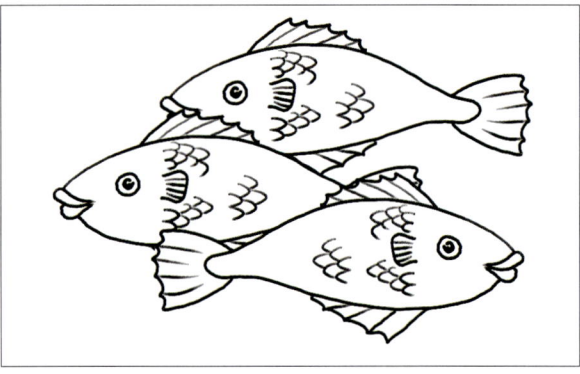

Copy and cut out cards for discussion and story sequencing activities.

What happens next?

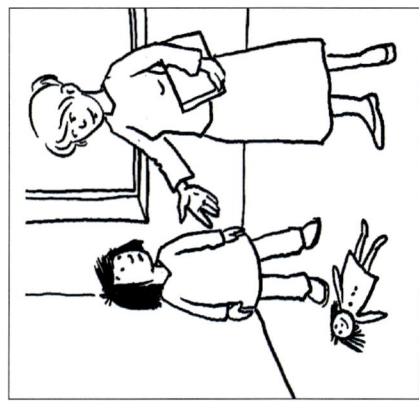

Theme: Good and bad behaviour

EYFS learning outcomes

To understand how we can:
- talk about our own and others' behaviour and its consequences
- know that some behaviour is unacceptable
- adjust our behaviour to different situations

What you need:

- Our special story and rhyme basket/box' (optional
- Please don't do that – poem
- Story board (optional)
- 'Please don't do that!' picture – Resource 1 (RS1)
- 'What did they do?' cards – Resource sheet 2 (RS2)
- 'Tower template' – Resource sheet 3 (RS3)

Getting ready:

Have a copy of the 'Please don't do that!' picture– RS1 available (or put it in 'Our special story and poem basket/box). You may want to use this poem for any issues that have happened during the day so that you can open a discussion with the children about it.

Introducing the poem

Show the 'Please don't do that!' picture to the children. Explain that it's playtime and a lot of the children are behaving in a bad way. Display the picture so the children can look at it as you read out or perform the poem.

Performance suggestions

Put emphasis on the verbs 'pull, kick, push, bite, pinch' as you read each verse. Use body language and facial expressions to highlight how you feel and to show the different actions.

Ideas to reinforce theme

- Discuss the bad behaviour in the poem with the children, e.g. hair pulling, kicking, pushing, biting and pinching. Ask: *Why are the children in the poem feeling upset?* Talk about what the children in the poem suggest the badly behaved child could do instead. Discuss other types of bad behaviour, such as hitting, snatching, name calling and why they are unacceptable.

- Display the 'What did they do?' cards – RS2. Look at each of the three bad behaviour pictures in turn and talk about why the behaviour is unacceptable. Point to the matching pictures and discuss the other children's reactions. Discuss different ways the children could deal with others being badly behaved towards them and how they could behave differently if they behaved badly. Highlight the importance of saying sorry.

Consolidation activities

Role play
Put the children into pairs. Give each pair a verse from the poem. Ask them to make up a scenario about the verse. What led up to the argument and how was it resolved? Emphasise that they must not actually physically hurt each other but just mime the actions.

Circle game
Ask the children in turn to say a bad behaviour that they don't like, e.g. '*I don't like shouting…. I don't like pinching…*'. Use the ideas to create new verses in the same style of the poem.

Use this game to highlight positive behaviour. Going clockwise, in turn, ask the children to think of one good things to say about the next child in the circle, e.g. something they have done, are good at, appearance etc.

Display idea
Display two large round faces (happy and grumpy faces). Add images of good behaviour around the smiley face and images of bad behaviour around the sad/grumpy face. Use the display as a talking point about behaviour with the children.

Please Don't Do That!

Please don't pull,
It really hurts my head.
If you really want to pull
Then pull a rope instead.

Please don't kick,
It really hurts my knee.
If you really want to kick
Then kick a ball to me.

Please don't push,
It really hurts my back.
If you really want to push
Then push a heavy sack.

Please don't bite,
It really hurts my thumb.
If you really want to bite
Then bite a juicy plum.

Please don't pinch,
It really hurts my hand.
If you really want to pinch
Then pinch a grain of sand.

Related activities within the learning environment

Literacy

Give out cut up copies of 'What did they do?' cards – RS2 to each child. Ask them to match the pairs and then colour in the images. Glue the pairs into little booklets or along a strip of paper for reference.

Have a recording of the poem, 'Please don't do that!' and a laminated copy of the 'Please don't do that!' picture – RS1 available so that the children can listen and look at the picture at the same time.

Mathematics

Give each child a copy of 'Tower template' - RS3 and two colouring pencils or counters – one for good behaviour and the other for bad behaviour. Describe a good or bad behaviour scenario. The children decide what it is and then use their good or bad behaviour colour on a tower brick.
Do several examples.

Art & Craft

Create large speech bubbles with good behaviour words in bubble fonts, e. g. *'Please'*, *'Thank you'*, *'Sorry!'* Read them out with the children and invite them to decorate them using shiny materials or bright colours. Display the words in mobiles or on display boards. Point to the words in class when needed.

Exploring

Give the children simple and easy-to-follow rules and instructions for using sand or water equipment to help discourage snatching, not sharing and arguments.

Model examples of how to treat each other and other living creatures with respect and care.

Music

Sing songs and rhymes as a springboard for discussion on good/bad behaviour, e.g. *Georgie Porgie, pudding and pie, There was a little girl* etc.

Use 'Tower template' - RS3 as a good behaviour chart for the class. Each time you see an example of good behaviour or someone saying sorry, add a happy sticker to a brick. Once the tower is covered in stickers, the children can have a treat such as a favourite story or game.

Small world

Set out play figures for the children to role-play different scenarios brought up from the poem and in subsequent discussion.

Use for discussion activities.

Please don't do that! Picture

Resource sheet 2

Copy and cut out.
Use for discussion and pairs activities.

Copy and cut out to use for activities.

Theme: Changes in routine

EYFS learning outcomes

To understand how we can:
- talk about how we and others show our feelings
- work as part of a group or class
- take changes of routine in our stride

What you need:

- Our special story and rhyme basket/box' (optional
- The Power Cut – story
- Story board (optional)
- Big white sheet or, whiteboard/ wall, torch or light beam (optional – see Getting ready)
- Shadow puppets (optional – see Getting ready)
- Shadow 'Rabbit and Tortoise' story board – Resource 1 (RS1)
- 'Changes in routine' cards – Resource sheet 2 (RS2)

Getting ready:

Before story time, set up the big white sheet or use a large white board/ wall. Close curtains or blinds and beam torches or lights onto the sheet/ board to create shadows.
Use Shadow 'Rabbit and Tortoise' story board – RS1 as a guide on how to make the rabbit and tortoise hand shapes. Practise the shadow story before performing to the children.

Introducing the story

Point to the white background and make a rabbit shadow with your hand. Ask the children what it is. Either let the rabbit shadow ask you to tell the children the story about Danielle and the power cut or highlight how you like making shadow animals like a girl called Danielle who learnt how to do them in a power cut. Check that the children know what a power cut is before you tell the story.

Performance suggestions

Within the main story is the retelling of Aesop's fable 'The Rabbit and the Tortoise'. Aim to learn the Aesop story by heart or in your own words so that you can perform it using the shadow images. At the end of the story, Danielle asks to do the story again. Use this as an invitation for the children to use their hands to make the rabbit and tortoise shadow shapes, while you perform the Aesop fable again. Model how you make the shapes with your fingers.

Ideas to reinforce theme

- Highlight how Danielle's normal evening at home suddenly changed because of the power cut. Ask what each family member was doing before the power cut. Ask: *What happened when the power went off? Why was Danielle nervous? What helped her stop worrying?* Encourage the children to share any experiences of power cuts in their home. Discuss what fun activities they could do in a power cut, e.g. play a word games, shadow play, tell jokes, etc.

- Talk about everyday routines in class or at home. Model a normal routine day for you. With the children, discuss the normal routine at school/group. Display the 'Changes in routine' cards – RS2. Look at each scenario and ask what has happened to change the child's normal routine. Encourage the children to share experiences and encourage them to talk about ways they would enjoy the situation or help them deal with it.

Consolidation activities

Role play
Ask the children to imagine they are at home and there is a power cut. Ask each of them to think of one thing they could do while there is no electricity. Encourage other children to join in with examples of songs, games or jokes.

Puppets
Let the children use their shadow stick puppets to re-create 'Old Macdonald had a farm' or 'Farmer's in his den' using a wide range of human characters, animals, objects created in an arts and craft session.

Game:
Play 'All change!' In an indoor or outdoor space, ask the children to mime or do actions and then create changes for them to adapt to, e.g. '*Time to sleep – Listen – a thunderstorm – all change – sing a song instead*'. '*Put on your sandals – oh no – it's raining – all change – put on your boots instead*.'

The Power Cut

It was a dark, wintry night and Danielle's family was happily settling down for the evening.

Danielle's mum was reading a book,
Danielle's dad was using the drill to put up a shelf,
Danielle's big brother was dancing to music on his new CD player,
Danielle's big sister was drying her hair with the hairdryer,
and Danielle was drawing a picture for her friend.

Suddenly everything went dark and quiet!
"Mum! Dad!" cried Danielle. "What's happening? The lights have gone out!"

"Don't worry. It's just a power cut," called out Danielle's dad. "I'll get some candles so that we can all see."

As her dad came in with the lit candles, big shadows began to appear on the living room walls. Danielle cuddled up to her mum on the sofa.

"I don't like power cuts!" she said nervously. "It's scary and dark."

Danielle's mum smiled.
"I know it's not the normal way we spend the evening but we can still have fun".

Danielle's brother jumped up in excitement.
"Let's do a shadow story on the wall." he suggested.
"Great," said Danielle's sister, but Danielle was not so sure.
"I don't want to look at scary shadows," she cried. "I want the lights back on."

Danielle's dad gave her a hug.
"We'll tell your favourite story about the race between the rabbit and the tortoise to make you feel better," he said kindly. "Sit with your mum and enjoy the show."

In the candlelight, Danielle's dad used his hands to make a shadow of a tortoise, and her sister made a shadow of a rabbit. As her brother told the story they made the tortoise and rabbit shadows move along the wall.

The Power Cut

One day, the rabbit met the tortoise plodding slowly along the road.

"Get out of my way, Tortoise!" shouted the rabbit. "You're too slow."

"I can beat you in a race any day," the tortoise replied.

They decided to have a race to find out who was the fastest.

Ready, steady, go…

The rabbit raced ahead quickly while the tortoise plodded slowly behind.

After a while the rabbit stopped and looked behind him.

"There's no way that silly tortoise can beat me," laughed the rabbit. "I'll have a quick nap before I win. There's plenty of time."

After a little while the tortoise plodded by the sleeping rabbit. He kept on plodding, slowly but steadily, towards the finishing line.

Suddenly the rabbit woke up. To his horror, he saw the tortoise about to cross the finishing line. He ran and ran as fast as he could.

Who would win the race?

It was very close at the finishing line but the winner was… the tortoise!'

Danielle cheered. "What a great shadow story," she said.

Suddenly all the lights came on. The power cut was over. Danielle quickly ran over to the light switch and turned the lights off again.

"I don't want the lights back on yet," she laughed. "I want to do the story again but this time, I'm going to be the rabbit."

We could do the same- Let's do the shadow story together.

Using storytelling to talk about…**Managing feelings & Behaviour**

Related activities within the learning environment

Literacy

Let the children draw a simple storyboard of their daily routine at home or in school. Let them do another day when it snows and they have to stay at home. What do they do instead? Encourage older children to write captions or simple sentences.

Set up a shadow puppet theatre for children to explore using their hand shapes or shape puppets to re-create the story. Suggest other stories such as Goldilocks etc.

Mathematics

Give the children different geometrical shapes to try on a shadow screen, Ask them to try combining the shadows to make new shapes. Encourage them to name the shapes.

Art & Craft

Leave out people, animal and object templates and thick black paper or card. Let children draw around the templates and cut them out (give support if needed). Attach sticks to the whole body or on limbs to make the move.

Give the children blank postcards. Ask the children to draw a picture of their favourite holiday or day trip. Write their address on the back and encourage them to copy out their name.

Exploring

Let the children explore using their arms, hands and fingers to make objects or creatures on the shadow screen. Encourage them to make their own stories using the shadows

Visitors & trips

Arrange a class trip. Highlight the differences in routine such as a picnic lunch or no story time.

Invite shadow puppeteers to visit or find a video telling a story with shadow puppets.

Role Play

Set up a dark corner using blankets. Leave out torches for the children to explore light and shadow. Discuss safety issues such as not shining the torch in others' eyes.

Resource sheet 1

Use for your own reference or cut up into cards for sequencing activities.

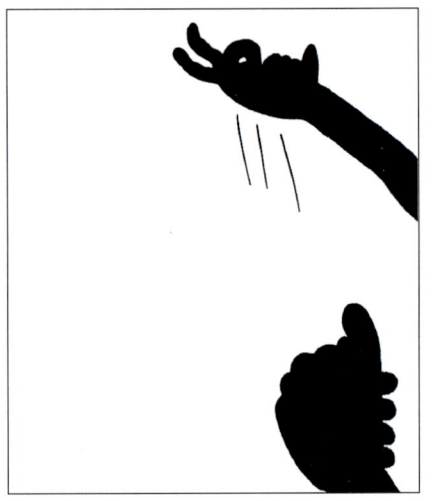  

Changes in routine cards

Copy and cut out the cards and use for discussion and activites.

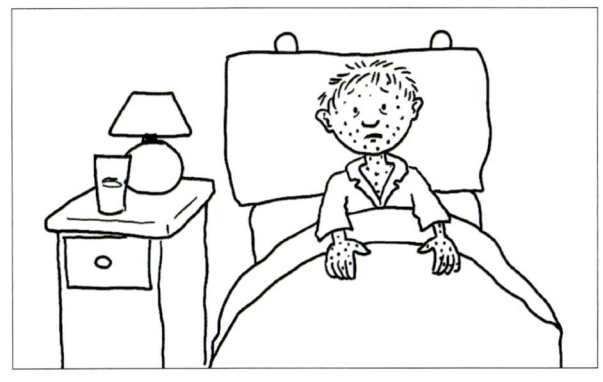

EYFS Learning Areas Reference Chart

Personal, social and emotional development								
	My Different Feelings	I've Lost My Blanket	There's a Monster Under My Bed	Hyena's Loud Laugh	Five Hungry Pirates	Listen, Becky Bear	Please Don't Do That!	The Power Cut
	Poem	Story	Poem	Story	Song	Story	Poem	Story
PERSONAL, SOCIAL AND EMOTIONAL DEVELOPMENT AREAS								
Managing feelings and behaviour								
To talk about how they and others show feelings	X	X	X	X			X	X
To talk about their own and others behaviour, and its consequences	X		X	X	X	X	X	
To know that some behaviour is unacceptable	X			X	X	X	X	
To understand and follow the rules					X	X	X	
To adjust their behaviour to different situations			X				X	X
To take changes of routine in their stride		X						X
OTHER PERSONAL, SOCIAL AND EMOTIONAL DEVELOPMENT AREAS								
Self-confidence and self-awareness	X	X	X				X	X
Making relationships	X			X	X		X	
OTHER LEARNING GOALS								
Communication and language	X	X	X	X	X	X	X	X
Physical development								
Literacy	X	X	X	X	X	X	X	X
Mathematics	X	X	X	X	X	X	X	X
Understanding the world	X				X		X	
Expressive arts and design	X	X	X	X	X	X	X	X

Storytelling assessment record

Personal, social and emotional development		
EYFS learning and development area: Theme: Story, poem or song: Title: Date:		
	OBSERVATIONS	IDEAS FOR NEXT SESSION
Preparation: learnt story/poem thoroughly; choice of props, resources, placement of resources before story time.		
Introduction: good use of anecdote or prop to introduce theme or story/poem/song; engagement and interaction of children; link into telling or performing main story/poem.		
Group/child engagement: eye contact; awareness of children with learning difficulties; held children's attention (all or parts); ability to cope with interruptions or unsettled behaviour. Flexibility in performance.		
Group interaction: join in with repetitive text, sounds; follow action movements; share and use props.		
Voice: clear and strong, use of voice tone and volume; use of voice to signal interactions or repetitive texts.		
Body language: Clear use of body actions to enhance performance.		
Pace and rhythm: clear start and ending of story; consistent pace of storytelling; clear difference in verse and chorus.		
Characters: use of different voices for different characters; use of voice to show moods and reactions; use of voice to emphasise rhythm.		
Ending of the session: Clear ending of session; good feedback and discussion from children about the story or poem/song.		

Observation suggestions

Title and theme	Observation suggestion
My Different Feelings – poem Theme: Dealing with feelings	• Listen to the different suggestions children make on how they deal with their different feelings. • Note how the children deal with their feelings within the learning environment.
I've Lost My Blanket! – story Theme: Losing something	• Do children share their experiences of how they coped with losing something special? Could they relate to the Little Prince? • Make notes of children who still need a special comforter with them in class.
There's a Monster Under My Bed – poem Theme; Feeling scared	• Are the children able to use the poem to discuss good strategies to help them deal with things that scare them? • Are the children able to talk about what scares them? Make notes of those children who may need extra support.
Hyena's Loud Laugh – story Theme: Being a good friend	• Do the children understand why Monkey and Elephant were not very good friends to Hyena? • Note examples of good friendship during the learning environment activities and praise the children involved.
Five Hungry Pirates – song Theme: Waiting your turn	• Do the children recognise different examples of when they may need to wait their turn and why? • Look for examples by the children of waiting in turn and lining up in class and outside of class.
Listen, Becky Bear! – story Theme: Learning to Listen	• Do the children understand why it was important for Becky Bear to listen to her dad? • Observe and praise good listening skills during story and poetry time.
Please Don't Do That! – poem Theme: Good and bad behaviour	• Listen to children share their experiences of good and bad behaviour. Do they recognise the examples of bad behaviour in the poem? • Make notes of improved behaviour by some children and also those who ask for help to deal with bad behaviour from others.
The Power Cut – story Theme: Changes in routine	• Note the children's shared experiences of how they felt when there was a change in routine and ways they dealt with it. • Observe children using puppets to role-play and tell imaginative stories with each other.

Observation record

Name/s *(child, pair or group)*:

Age/s:

Story or poem/song title:

Main learning outcomes:

Child/children's understanding and comments about the main theme in the story or poem/song:

Further activities observations, e.g. how are the children showing what they've learnt in other activities and day-to-day relationships?

Further support or needs: